# THE JAMESTOWN COLONY

Turning Points
IN AMERICAN HISTORY

# THE JAMESTOWN COLONY

*Carter Smith*

Silver Burdett Press, Inc.

*Acknowledgments*

The author and editor thank the following people for their invaluable help in text and picture research: Kurt Stallings, National Park Service, Colonial National Historical Park; Mikell Brown and Carolyn S. Parsons, Virginia State Library and Archives; and Howell W. Perkins, Virginia Museum of Fine Arts.

*Consultants*

We thank the following people for reviewing the manuscript and offering their helpful suggestions:

Robert M. Goldberg
Consultant to the Social Studies Department (formerly
  Department Chair)
Oceanside Middle School
Oceanside, New York

Richard M. Haynes
Assistant Professor
Division of Administration, Instruction,
  and Curriculum
Western Carolina University
Cullowhee, North Carolina

*Cover: The Jamestown colonists begin building their fort in April 1607. From a series of paintings by Sidney King, reproduced through the courtesy of the National Park Service.*

*Title Page: This nineteenth-century painting is titled* The Hope of Jamestown. *Virginia Museum of Fine Arts.*

*Contents Page: This 1609 book was published to encourage settlement in Virginia. The Bettmann Archive.*

*Back Cover: John Smith, one of Jamestown's early leaders. Virginia State Library.*

Library of Congress Cataloging-in-Publication Data

Smith, Carter.
   The Jamestown Colony / Carter Smith
        p.    cm. — (Turning Points in American history)
   Includes bibliographical references (p. 64) and index.
   Summary: Describes the founding of Jamestown, Virginia, and the
struggle of the colonists to survive in the New World.
        1. Jamestown (Va.)—History—Juvenile literature. 2. Virginia—
History—Colonial period, ca. 1600-1775—Juvenile literature.
   [1. Jamestown (Va.)—History. 2. Virginia—History—Colonial
period, ca. 1600-1775.]            I. Title.    II. Series.
        F234.J3S65 1991
        975.5' 562—dc20
                                                    91-2537
                                                    CIP
                                                    AC

Editorial Coordination by Richard G. Gallin

 Created by Media Projects Incorporated

Carter Smith, *Executive Editor*
Charles A. Wills, *Series Editor*
Bernard Schleifer, *Design Consultant*
Arlene Goldberg, *Cartographer*

ISBN 0-382-24121-5 [lib. bdg.]
10 9 8 7 6 5 4 3 2 1

ISBN 0-382-24116-9 [pbk.]
10 9 8 7 6 5 4 3 2 1

OFFERING MOST Excellent fruites by Planting in VIRGINIA.

Exciting all such as be well affected to further the same.

LONDON
Printed for SAMVEL MACHAM, and are to be sold at his Shop in Pauls-Church-yard, at the Signe of the Bul-head.
1609.

# CONTENTS

# INTRODUCTION

---

# JUNE 1610: THE DESPERATE EVACUATION, THE BRAVE RETURN

**I**n April 1607, 105 Englishmen braved the Atlantic Ocean and arrived in "The New World." They landed at the mouth of a river they called the James, after the king of England, James I. They named the land Virginia after Elizabeth, England's unmarried queen, who had died four years before. Their aim was to plant an English colony in North America. But by June 1610, the colonists' situation was so desperate that they were giving up. They decided to try to get back to England.

It had been a struggle from the start. The "factory fort" that the colonists had built was on a low and marshy peninsula about thirty miles up Chesapeake Bay from the ocean. It was well situated

*A settler doles out part of his meager supply of corn during the "starving time."*

for defense against Native American (Indian) attacks but not against swarms of disease-carrying mosquitoes from the surrounding swamps.

At first the Native Americans and the colonists got along well. But as the white men ventured farther inland, the Indians came to resent the invaders. Fighting broke out, with many dead among both the colonists and the local tribes.

But the biggest problem for the new colony was its failure to plant crops of corn and vegetables and raise livestock for food. Hunger soon stalked Jamestown.

The colony grew to almost seven hundred people with later arrivals from England. By the fall of 1609, however, only about four hundred men, women, and children remained alive. Starvation,

*Lord De La Warr's rescue fleet reaches Jamestown.*

disease, and conflict with the Indians had taken a heavy toll. Then came the cruel killing winter of 1609—the "Starving Time."

Even before the cold had set in, the food in the colony's storehouse had been exhausted. The supplies of corn traded from the Indians of the Powhatan Confederacy ceased. Perhaps sensing that the colonists might be forced to abandon Jamestown, the Indians stepped up attacks.

In Jamestown the colonists broke up empty houses to make fires to warm themselves. Men desperately traded clothing and blankets for a little corn.

Death came from freezing as well as famine. Settlers driven mad by cold and hunger started eating boots, shoes, snails, lizards, and tree bark.

But the most gruesome acts came as the winter ended. According to colonist and chronicler John Smith, desperate, starving colonists dug up corpses from their graves and "ravenously ate them . . . stewed with roots and herbs."

The colony's leader was George Percy, "an old planter of the highest social rank," who could barely maintain discipline among the colonists. He himself was, in the spelling of the day, "so sicke hee could neither goe nor stand."

But in May, Percy realized that the sixty surviving colonists might have a better chance if their company moved down to Point Comfort on the Atlantic coast.

He was on the verge of moving the colony when two small ships came into sight. They carried survivors of the shipwreck of the *Sea Venture*, a relief ship that had set out from England a year before. The *Sea Venture* had sunk near the Bermuda islands, and the survivors had built the two vessels from its wreckage. Unfortunately, the newcomers had brought no food. Now Jamestown had even more mouths to feed. One of the newcomers, Sir Thomas Gates, took command.

A check of supplies showed only enough to feed the survivors for sixteen days. Gates decided to put the half-starved settlers in four small ships and sail up the coast to Newfoundland, an island off Canada's eastern coast. There he hoped to find an English fishing fleet to carry the colonists home to England.

On June 7, 1610, about two hundred men, women, and children sailed away from Jamestown. But in one of the most important turning points in American history, the sails of a small boat suddenly appeared on the horizon. The boat had been sent from a rescue fleet commanded by Lord De La Warr, Virginia's new governor. With him were three hundred healthy passengers and a year's supply of provisions.

According to some accounts, the surviving settlers voted to return to their recently deserted colony. Other sources say Lord De La Warr ordered the return. In either case, England's attempt to plant its first permanent colony in North America hadn't failed after all.

# 1

## THE NEW WORLD

From the beginning of recorded history, people have looked for new lands to conquer. In the beginning, new lands meant the next clearing, or across the river, or the other side of the mountain. Later, this involved longer-range hunting and food-gathering explorations. Later still, seafaring peoples crossed seas and oceans in search of richer lands—or sometimes just for the adventure of it. Of course, each place people went was equally ancient; it was new only to the explorers.

The land we call North America was no exception. Most archaeologists and historians believe the continent has been populated by human beings for at least eleven thousand years. Between Five and Nine million people lived in what is now the United States and Canada when the first European explorers arrived.

*Christopher Columbus lands in the New World on October 12, 1492.*

European exploration across the stormy Atlantic Ocean began as early as 986, when Scandinavians, the Viking seamen, reached Greenland, a huge island in the North Atlantic. From Greenland other Vikings, including Leif Ericsson, explored parts of what is now eastern Canada, including Labrador and Newfoundland. The Vikings set up a colony on Newfoundland that lasted for about three years. More than four centuries would pass, however, before Europeans again ventured to North America.

During this time, western European society was *feudal*. Under feudalism, most of the people lived on small farms, growing just enough food to survive. Governments were mostly local, with a handful of "nobles" ruling small territories. But by the 1400s, the feudal system began to give way to a more "national" form of government. The monarchs of Portugal, Spain, France, and England gained much central control over their populations.

The economies of these nations were still mostly based on agriculture, but single-family farms were being replaced by farming for profit. Europe's cities were growing, creating a new middle class of craftspeople and merchants who were prosperous enough to afford a few luxuries. Among these luxuries were spices. There was no way to keep meat fresh at this time, so spices were used to make half-spoiled meat tasty. The only place to get spices—and the silks, perfumes, and other goods people wanted—was the Orient (Asia). The Orient was also called "the Indies," from India. To get to the Orient, traders had to travel the long way—by land across Europe and the Middle East.

In the fifteenth and early sixteenth centuries, the Turkish Empire captured Constantinople and Cairo, key cities on the overland trade routes to the Orient. The Turks placed heavy taxes on the trade caravans passing through their lands. Also, European nations had to pay fees to Italian city-states, like Venice and Genoa, that controlled sea trade on the Mediterranean Sea. To avoid these obstacles, the European states needed to find new sea routes to the riches of the East.

The first to achieve success was Portugal, a small nation on Europe's western Atlantic coast. Led by young Prince Henry, "The Navigator," Portugal had already founded settlements on the Azores and Madeira Islands in the Atlantic and had opened up trade with Africa. By the end of the 1400s, Portuguese trading ships had reached India by sailing south and then east around Africa's southern tip.

The discovery that was to change the course of history came in 1492. In that year, Christopher Columbus, a sailor from Italy, sailed across the Atlantic Ocean and "discovered" America.

Columbus's expedition, which was sponsored by Spain's monarchs Ferdinand and Isabella, was based on a revolutionary idea. By sailing west into waters unexplored by Europeans, Columbus hoped to reach Asia by going around the earth.

On October 12, 1492, Columbus's three ships (the *Niña*, the *Pinta*, and the *Santa María*) sighted an island in what is now the Bahamas. Sailing on, he reached the islands of Cuba and Hispaniola.

When Columbus's flagship, the *Santa María*, went aground off Hispaniola, Columbus built a fort and left forty-four men of his crew to establish Spain in "the Indies." He sailed back to Spain aboard the *Nina*, bringing gold, precious stones, and other products of the lands he had found. Until his death in 1506, Columbus believed these lands were the East Indies near Japan, on the other side of the world. For this reason, the inhabitants of the lands he discovered came to be called "Indians."

Soon all Europe was talking about the great riches to be found in the "New World." These stories inspired the "age of discovery." Many explorers sailed from Spain and Portugal seeking riches across the Atlantic.

One of these explorers was Amerigo

*Ferdinand Magellan navigates through the strait that bears his name in 1520.*

Vespucci, also an Italian. He made several voyages to the New World under the sponsorship of King Ferdinand of Spain and, later, King Emanuel of Portugal. After his 1499 expedition, Vespucci claimed to have discovered North America—which many historians doubt. But the claim alone made him immortal, because the continents to the west were soon shown on maps as *America*, from his name, Amerigo. Vespucci suggested that the Orient might be reached by sailing around the southern tip of South America.

In 1519 an expedition led by Ferdinand Magellan, under the sponsorship of Charles I of Spain, became the first to circumnavigate (sail completely around) the world. News of this extraordinary voyage spread among the European mapmakers. Now the nature of the great new continents that separated Europe from Asia was clear.

Many Spanish explorers—often called *conquistadors*, from "conqueror" in Spanish—now journeyed across the Atlantic to the New World.

In 1518, Hernando Cortés led an expedition to Mexico, destroying the great Aztec civilization there and claiming the land for Spain. Farther south, on the west coast of South America—modern-day Peru—Francisco Pizzaro conquered the empire of the Incas in much the same way.

By the middle of the sixteenth century Spain ruled the Caribbean Sea and the Gulf of Mexico. The mainland and islands that touched these seas, plus Peru, gave Spain an empire larger than all Europe.

The riches from that empire made Spain the dominant nation In Europe. In a single year, 1512, Spanish ships brought about $1 million in gold back to the home country—a huge sum at that time. Eventually, silver from the great mine at Potosí in Bolivia and from mines in Mexico, replaced gold as Spain's chief source of wealth.

The treasure carried a cruel price for the natives of the New World. The conquistadors butchered and plundered the peoples they conquered. The Carib Indians in the Indies, the Aztec and Mayan nations in Mexico, the Chibara in Colombia, and the Inca of Peru all were virtually wiped out.

Spanish explorers soon became interested in the lands to the north of Mexico—the region that would become the United States.

The first Spanish explorer to land in this region was Juan Ponce de León, a Spanish nobleman. Ponce de León reached Florida in 1513. He had been drawn to North America by stories of a mythical "fountain of youth." Ponce de León gave Florida its name (possibly because of the beautiful plants—*flora*—that grew there), but he found no fountain. Returning to colonize the west

coast of Florida in 1521, he was killed by a Native American arrow.

The North American southeast was next visited by the Spanish in 1528, when Pánfilo de Narváez landed near Tampa Bay. The expedition met with a series of disasters, including Narváez's death, but a handful of survivors journeyed by foot across the south to what is now Galveston, Texas, and finally to Mexico City. That venture was followed in 1539 by one led by Hernando de Soto, who landed in Florida with six hundred men and moved west seeking gold. De

*A painting by artist Frederic Remington shows Coronado's expedition on the march.*

Soto died in 1542, and the expedition's survivors wandered through Florida and what are today the states of Alabama, Mississippi, Louisiana, Tennessee, and Georgia before returning to Mexico.

About the same time a large Spanish expedition led by Francisco Vásquez de Coronado moved north from Mexico City in search of Cibola, seven cities of gold that the Indians kept telling the Europeans about. Instead, Coronado discovered the pueblo cities of the Zuni people and the Grand Canyon.

The Spanish were the most active and successful colonizers of the New World, not only because of their early voyages but also thanks to a decree (*bull*) made by Pope Alexander VI in 1493. The pope decreed that Spain and Portugal would share all the land in the New World. Portugal was granted Brazil and the Atlantic Islands; Spain gained all the rest.

The rest of Europe, excluded by this papal bull, could not be kept from the New World for long, however. France, Holland, and England all disregarded

*John Cabot, an Italian navigator sailing for England, reached North America in 1497.*

the pope's decree and sent their explorers westward across the Atlantic.

In 1497, an Italian, Giovanni Caboto, who had changed his name to John Cabot, sailed west under the English flag. After fifty-two days at sea, Cabot reached Cape Breton Island, off the coast of Canada, and became the first explorer to plant the English flag in America. Four years later, another small English expedition reached Labrador and Newfoundland.

The first French expedition to the New World came in 1534, when Jacques Cartier explored Canada's Gulf of St. Lawrence for France. He returned in 1535 and spent the winter with friendly Huron Indians. The Hurons, like their fellow storytellers in the south, told Cartier about a rich kingdom farther west.

On a third voyage, in 1541, Cartier collected "fool's gold" (a worthless mineral that looks like gold) and crystals that he believed to be diamonds. Back in France, he became a laughingstock for these finds. To the south at Parris Island (now part of South Carolina) in 1562, a French colony was established by Jean Ribault. The colonists were not able to survive by farming and hunting and returned to France the next year.

By now, religion was beginning to play a role in events in the New World. In 1517, a German monk named Martin Luther spoke out against what he saw as corruption in the Roman Catholic Church. This began the era of the Reformation. Over the next few years, much of northern Europe followed the lead of Luther and other reformers and denied the authority of the pope. From their "protest" against the pope, these people became known called Protestants. In the 1530s, King Henry VIII of England, angry because the pope refused to grant him a divorce, declared England a Protestant nation.

By the 1540s, the Reformation had drawn a battle line—political as well as religious—across Europe. The conflict quickly spread to America. Spain and Portugal, which had remained Catholic, tried hard to keep Protestants out of the New World. However, Protestant minorities in Catholic countries wanted to found colonies where they could practice their religion freely. One such group were the French Protestants, the Huguenots.

In 1564, a Huguenot colonizing expedition founded Fort Caroline in northern Florida. Alarmed by French colonization in "their" territory, Spain established a colony at St. Augustine in Florida. It was to be the first permanent European settlement in America.

A few months after establishing his fort at St. Augustine, the Spanish commander, Admiral Pedro Menéndez de Avilés, attacked the French outpost at Fort Caroline. The Spanish overwhelmed the fort and slaughtered almost every man, woman, and child in the colony—leaving a sign proclaiming, "I do this not to Frenchmen, but to Lutherans [Protestants]."

Word of the Spanish massacre of the French Protestants in Florida reached England with some of the few survivors. The English were angry at the Spanish commander's cruelty. They were also envious of the wealth brought to Spain by its colonies.

Religion, European politics, the lure of gold, and trade routes—all these things played major roles in the exploration and settlement of the New World. By 1565, despite the efforts of England and France, Spain remained the major European presence in the new golden land, with an empire including Florida and the southwest in North America. And while France had been driven from Florida, that nation had laid the foundation for later settlements to the north, in the land that became Canada. But between Canada and Florida lay a vast stretch of territory, visited only by Verrazano and a handful of other explorers. England would soon turn its attention to this land.

Engraved for
Middleton's Complete
System of Geography.

SIR WALTER RALEIGH ordering the STANDARD
of Queen Elizabeth to be erected on the Coast
of VIRGINIA.

Taylor delin.          sculp.

# 2

## A DUEL FOR THE NEW WORLD

The age of Queen Elizabeth I who ruled England from 1558–1603, was one of the most creative periods in the history of the world. Christopher Marlowe, a playwright of the day, called it "an age of wonder and delight."

It was the age that gave us the work of William Shakespeare, the greatest writer of the English language, and poets like Ben Jonson and Edmund Spenser. It was the age when Francis Bacon was writing brilliant essays and Walter Raleigh and Richard Hakluyt were writing exciting accounts of history and discovery.

It is also remembered as the age in which the diplomacy of "Good Queen

*An engraving from an early geography textbook shows Sir Walter Raleigh planting the English flag in Virginia. Actually, Raleigh never set foot in the colony he helped establish.*

Bess" and her ministers, and the bravery of her admirals and generals, shaped the future of North America.

Already jealous of the vast treasures Spain was reaping in the New World, Elizabeth and her counselors wondered if England could colonize North America. After all, Protestant England didn't recognize Pope Alexander VI's decree granting the New World to Portugal and Spain.

By the middle of the sixteenth century, a remarkable group of English sailors appeared on the world's oceans. England was a small island nation. It was only natural that it would turn to the sea in search of wealth. England's sixteenth-century seafarers, including John Hawkins and Francis Drake, made their voyages in search of treasure. Still, they explored much of the world and paved the way for England's colonization of North America. To the Spanish, whose ships and colonies they plundered, England's seafarers were pirates. To Queen Elizabeth and the English people, however, they were brave adventurers who brought riches home to their small country.

In 1567, English Captain John Hawkins, a slave trader, began a fateful voyage. With five ships, he sailed to the coast of Mexico. A storm forced him to seek shelter in the Spanish port of Vera Cruz. Then a fleet of thirteen ships from Spain appeared.

The Spanish commander guaranteed Hawkins the safety of the harbor, but Hawkins's small fleet was treacherously attacked. Hawkins lost three of his ships. The other two got out to sea, but with so little food that the crews were forced to eat rats, dogs, and boiled parrots. Luckily for England, the captain of one of the two ships that made it back to England was Francis Drake.

Drake wanted revenge and profit— for himself and for Queen Elizabeth, who had invested in his expeditions. He began a series of voyages to plunder the Spanish colonies in the New World.

In 1577, Drake sailed from Plymouth, England, with five ships. He intended to sail around South America and strike at the Spanish outposts on the continent's Pacific coast.

Only Drake's flagship, the *Golden Hind*, made it through to the Pacific. Undaunted, Drake sailed north up the coast of Chile and Peru, dashing into Spanish ports and taking away enormous treasure in gold, silver, and jewels.

Reaching the coast of what is now California, Drake went ashore and took possession of what he named New Albion. (Albion is another name for England.)

In 1936, a young man camping by San Francisco Bay picked up a small brass plate engraved with this message:

Bee it known unto all men by these presents
June 17 1579
By the grace of God and in the name of Herr Maiesty Queen Elizabeth of England and her successors forever I take possession of this kingdome whose king and people freely resigne their right and title to the whole land unto her maiesties keepeing now named by me an to bee knowne unto all men as Nova Albion.
Francis Drake.

Some people felt the discovery was a fake, but scientific dating of the metal confirmed its age.

Drake sailed on across the Pacific and around the tip of Africa, landing at Plymouth in September 1580. As the first Englishman to sail around the world, Drake was knighted—made Sir Francis Drake—by Queen Elizabeth.

Drake's exploit brought riches for England's treasury. It also brought great pride to the English people. A year later, in 1581, Elizabeth made a direct challenge to Spain: "The Spaniards have brought these evils on themselves by their injustice towards the English, whom they have excluded from commerce with the West Indies (That is America). The Queen does not acknowledge that her subjects and those of other nations may be excluded from the Indies. . . ."

While Hawkins, Drake, and others were bringing home Spanish gold, others in England began looking at the New World as a business opportunity. They saw American colonies as places where England's poor and unemployed could go to start new lives. If successful colonies could be established in America, England would benefit in two ways. The colonists would ship valuable materials—fur, timber, minerals—back to England. In return, the settlers would buy English manufactured goods. There were other reasons for England's interest in overseas colonies. One of them was religion: Protestant England wanted to limit Catholic Spain's influence in America. And, as always, there was the hope of finding precious metals or a new route to Asia.

The two most important promoters of English colonies in North America were Sir Humphrey Gilbert and his half brother, Walter Raleigh. In 1578, Gilbert obtained a patent from Queen Elizabeth "to inhabit and possess at his choice all remote and heathen lands not in actual possession of a Christian prince." (A patent was the right to explore and colonize a specific area.) Gilbert succeeded in taking possession of Newfoundland, a large island off Canada's eastern coast, in 1583. But no permanent colony was founded, and later that year Gilbert died in a storm while returning to England. The royal patent passed to Walter Raleigh.

*Queen Elizabeth I knights Francis Drake after his voyage around the world.*

Raleigh was a writer, soldier, and explorer as well as a promoter of colonies. One nineteenth-century historian characterized him as the "pioneering genius" who "led Great Britain to dot the world with her colonies and to become for several centuries the greatest power on earth." In 1584, Raleigh planned to establish a colony on the coast of North America.

*Sir Walter Raleigh (or Ralegh, as it was sometimes spelled).*

According to Raleigh's patent, his colonists were to have "all the privileges of free persons . . . native to England." They were to be governed "according to such statutes as shall be by him [Raleigh] or them established." This "local government" phrase proved to be important in the eighteenth century, when England's American colonies moved toward independence.

On April 27, 1584, Raleigh sent two ships, captained by Philip Amadas and Arthur Barlowe, on an exploring expedition. In early July, the colonists landed on an island off the coast of what is now North Carolina. The entire region was given the name Virginia.

On the island, which they called Roanoke, from the Indian name Ohganoak, the explorers found the Native Americans to be "very handsome and goodly people, and in their behavior as mannerly and civill as any of Europe."

After two months the expedition returned to England. The explorers reported finding a beautiful land filled with friendly Indians, abundant fish and game, and soil that was "the most plentiful, sweete, fruitfull, and wholsome of all the worlde."

A few months later, Raleigh sent a fleet of seven ships and about a hundred settlers to found a permanent colony on Roanoke. The fleet's commander was Sir Richard Grenville, Raleigh's cousin. The colony's governor was Ralph Lane.

After landing on July 27, 1585, Lane's men built a fort and houses. Grenville returned to England for more supplies.

The colonists spent much of their time looking for gold. They did make one long exploration up a river the Indians said reached across the continent. This "Northwest Passage"—an easy route to the riches of Asia—was a favorite goal of European explorers. Unfortunately, the river ended only a few miles inland.

Soon, supplies began to run out. The colonists had depended on the Indians for food, but relations between the English and the Indians became unfriendly. In 1586, war broke out between the colonists and the Indians.

In that same year, Sir Francis Drake appeared at Roanoke with a twenty-

*John White painted this scene of Indians catching fish with spears and traps.*

*John White's map of what is now the coast of North Carolina.*

three-ship fleet. He was on his way home after raiding Spanish colonies in the Caribbean.

Having lost hope of Grenville's return, Lane and the colonists jumped at the chance to sail back to England with Drake. The first Roanoke colony had lasted less than a year.

Three weeks later, Grenville did arrive. Finding the fort deserted, he sailed home, leaving fifteen men behind to maintain England's claim. When another expedition reached Roanoke the next year, it found only the men's bones.

This expedition, which landed in

# PICTURES OF THE NEW WORLD:
## The Watercolors of John White

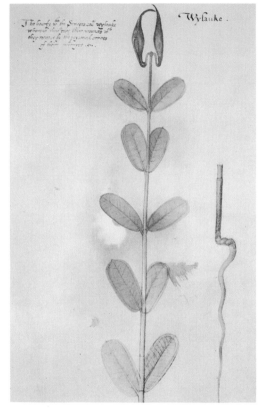

A milkweed plant. According to the notes White wrote for the picture, Indians used the plant's leaves to soothe arrow wounds.

A flamingo.

A tiger swallow-tail butterfly.

Little is known about John White's life up to the time he sailed to North America with the first Roanoke colonists in 1585. White spent only a short time in Virginia before returning to England, but during his brief stay he made many remarkable sketches and paintings of the people, plants, and animals around the settlement at Roanoke. White also drew a number of maps that proved valuable to later explorers and settlers.

In 1587, White returned to Virginia as governor of the second Roanoke colony. However, he again returned to England, this time because the settlers wanted him to personally ask for more supplies for the colony. Unfortunately, several years passed before White could return to Virginia. When he did, he discovered the entire colony had disappeared. Among the vanished colonists was White's daughter, Eleanor Dare, and his granddaughter, Virginia. White finally moved to Ireland, where he died, probably in 1593.

White's artwork is historically important as well as beautiful. It shows North America as the first Europeans saw it, less than a century after Columbus's first voyage.

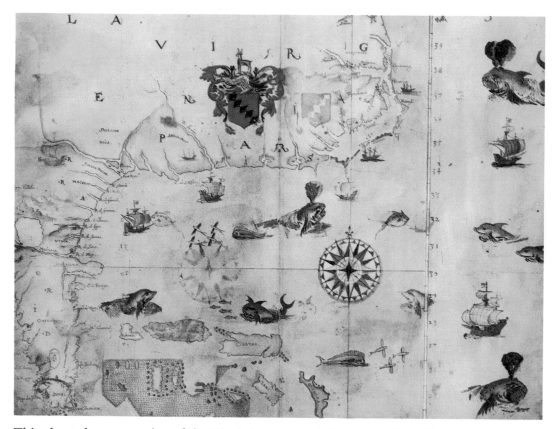

*This chart shows a section of the Virginia coast and Chesapeake Bay. Places where White landed are marked by red dots.*

*A relief expedition reached Roanoke in 1591, only to discover that the entire colony had disappeared, as depicted in this later engraving.*

July 1587, consisted of ninety-one men, seventeen women, and nine children. Their governor was Captain John White. White was a talented artist, and his watercolors of the new land's plants, animals, and people stirred much later interest in colonization. White's daughter, Eleanor White Dare, was among the colonists. In August, she gave birth to a baby girl named Virginia Dare—the first English child born in North America. Shortly after Virginia's birth, Governor White sailed back to England for supplies. It would be four years before he could return.

Unfortunately, Roanoke was destined to become known as the "lost colony." No one knows just what happened to the colonists. Four years later, another expedition found the colony deserted. The only clue to the fate of the colonists was the word *Croatoan* carved into a tree. Some historians believe that conflict with the nearby Indians led the colonists to try to escape to the friendly Croatoan tribe. On the way, they may have been massacred. According to a stone found in North Carolina, possibly written by one of the survivors, all but seven of the colonists were killed. The survivors may have been adopted by other Indians.

Even after two unsuccessful attempts, Sir Walter Raleigh remained convinced "I shall yet live to see an English nation" in America. But Queen Elizabeth died in 1603, and Raleigh fell out of favor with Elizabeth's successor, King James I. Raleigh was eventually executed in 1618. True to his words, however, he died knowing that an English colony, Jamestown, had been planted in Virginia.

The Roanoke colony might not have been lost if more supplies and settlers had reached Roanoke. But events at home took England's attention away from the struggling colony.

By the 1580s, England's poor relations with Spain reached the point of war. Spainish leaders grew angry when England aided Protestant rebels in Holland, which was ruled by Catholic Spain. The conflict soon led England's seafarers to sail against Spain.

Sir Francis Drake had plenty of experience in attacking Spain's colonies. In 1587, he struck at Spain itself. In April of that year, Drake sailed to the Spanish coast and destroyed thirty-seven ships in Cadiz harbor. (Spain admitted losing twenty-four.)

Drake's fleet wasn't strong enough to attack the huge fleet that King Philip II was preparing for an attack on England. Drake's comment was that he had only "singed the King of Spain's beard." The great Spanish fleet, called the Armada, was to carry Spanish troops to invade England. In May 1588, the fleet of about 130 vessels set sail from Spain and Portugal.

The Armada's mission was a failure. Although the Spanish ships made it to France, the English fleet, led by Sir Francis Drake, kept it bottled up in the harbor at Calais. The Spanish invasion force, which the Armada was supposed to land in England, was tied down in Holland. Finally, low on supplies and weary of attacks by English warships, the Spanish admiral Medina Sedonia headed back to Spain. The Armada tried to avoid the English fleet by sailing around the north coasts of Scotland and Ireland. Unfortunately, a huge storm wrecked many of the Spanish ships on the rocky coast.

England was now in command of the world's oceans. Spain remained a powerful force in both Europe and the New World, but now neither Spain nor any other nation could stop England's plans for a colonial empire.

# 3

---

# A MEETING—AND A CLASH—OF CULTURES

Raleigh's failure to found a permanent colony in North America didn't discourage ambitious English nobles, merchants, and seafarers. After England made peace with Spain in the early 1600s, the nation was free to turn its attention to the lands across the Atlantic.

Treasure remained the chief lure. In 1605, a comedy play called *Eastward Ho!* opened on a London stage. The play looked on America as the road to China, where ". . . all their dripping pans are pure gold . . . all the prisoners they take are fettered [chained] in gold; and the rubies and diamonds, they go forth on holidays and gather 'em up by the seashore." But it was fish, not gold, that brought the next expedition to America from England.

*Opechancanough, brother of Powhatan and one of the leaders of the Virginia Indians.*

Since the 1490s, English shipmasters had competed with the French, Spanish, and Portuguese for fish and whales in the waters off what is now eastern Canada. In 1602, Bartholomew Gosnold explored the North American coast from present-day Maine to Martha's Vineyard. (He named this island off Massachusetts after his daughter.) Gosnold also brought back reports of huge schools of fish "for the taking." He tried to establish a trading outpost, but the men he left behind eventually returned to England.

The merchants of England's growing cities and ports realized there was plenty of money to be made from fishing and trade. As early as 1553, a company called the "Merchant Adventurers for the Discovery of Regions, Dominions, Islands, and Places Unknown" had been established. This company and the ones that followed hoped to profit by backing expeditions to the

*This seal of King James was placed on the charter of the Virginia Company.*

New World. In 1606, two new companies were created: the Virginia Company of London, and the Virginia Company of Plymouth. (At the time, all the land along North America's Atlantic coast was called "Virginia" by the English.) Their purpose was to establish permanent colonies "of our people into that part of America called Virginia."

Although each company received a charter (royal permission to operate) from King James, they were organized as private businesses. Both were joint-stock companies. People bought shares of each company's stock, providing the money needed to set up the colonies. If a colony was successful, profits would be divided among the company's shareholders—those who had bought shares of stock. Many people, from the king to ordinary London merchants, invested in these ventures. They hoped that the colonizing expeditions would find gold or precious minerals, or trade with Virginia's inhabitants for furs and other valuable products.

Each company was given a certain area to colonize, and neither company could establish a colony within one hundred miles of the other. The Virginia Company of Plymouth, known as the Plymouth Company, had the right to plant a colony in the land between the thirty-eighth and forty-fifth parallels of latitude—an area that stretches from the middle of modern-day Pennsylvania to Maine.

The Virginia Company of London, which became better known as the Virginia Company, was to plant its colony to the north of the thirty-fourth parallel, which runs across what is now South Carolina. The northern border of the company's grant was the forty-first parallel, which today crosses the states of New York, New Jersey, and Pennsylvania. There was no western border; the charter gave the company territory across the continent "to the South Sea" (Pacific Ocean). The Virginia Company's royal charter lists "Sir Thomas Gates and Sir George Somers, Knights, Richard Hakluyt, Clerk of Westminster, Edward-Maria Wingfield, and other knights, gentlemen, merchants, and adventurers" as founding members.

The king's charter created the Council of Virginia in London to oversee the colony. There would be a lesser council in the colony itself. The council in Virginia would have the power to coin money, import settlers, drive out invaders, punish criminals, and collect taxes.

*The* Susan Constant, *the* Godspeed, *and the* Discovery *arrive at the coast of Virginia on April 26, 1607.*

The local council, according to the charter, was to govern the colonies "as near to the common laws of England" as possible.

The Plymouth Company sent two ships, the *Mary and John* and the *Gift of God*, to New England (then called North Virginia) in 1607. The expedition built a fort and church on the banks of the Kennebec River in what is now Maine. But the usual miseries suffered by early colonists—sickness, starvation, a freezing winter—followed. Those colonists who survived until the summer of 1608 returned home.

The Virginia Company's first expedition left England on December 19, 1606. It consisted of three ships: the *Susan Constant*, captained by Christopher Newport (who was also commander of the small fleet), with 71 people aboard; the *Godspeed*, carrying 52 people, under Captain Bartholomew Gosnold; and the little *Discovery*, captained by John Ratcliffe, with only 20 aboard.

Of the men aboard the ships, 39 were crew who would return to England. The rest—105 men—were to stay behind as colonists. Of these, about half were listed as "gentlemen." One was a "chirurgeon" (surgeon), and another, Reverend Robert Hunt, a Church of England (Protestant) minister. Among the rest were four carpenters, two blacksmiths, a tailor, twelve "laborers," and four boys.

The three ships set a southwest course and reached the Virginia coast on April 26, dropping anchor in Chesapeake Bay.

During the voyage, a small sealed box had been kept aboard the *Susan Constant*. Now it was opened. The document inside it revealed the names of the councilors (leaders) of the Virginia Company as appointed by the royal charter. They included Captains Newport, Gosnold, and Ratcliffe, and Edward-Maria Wingfield, John Martin, John Kendall, and John Smith. These men would govern the new colony of Jamestown, named for the king of England. The newly appointed council elected Wingfield as its president. It also voted to exclude John Smith from the council.

Smith was a truly remarkable man. He was born around 1580 in rural Lincolnshire, England, and his formal education ended at age fifteen. Then he left home to become an apprentice (craftsman in training) to a merchant. Like many young Englishmen of the day, however, Smith hoped to go to sea.

Unable to a find a ship to sail in, Smith went to Holland. There he became a soldier for the Dutch Protestants fighting the forces of Spain. In 1600, Smith decided that he "was desirous to see more of the world and trie my fortune against the Turks." He traveled to Hungary and became a cavalry captain in the Austrian army, which was fighting Muslim invaders from Turkey.

Then Smith was captured by the Turks. He was sent to the Turkish capital, Constantinople, to be sold into slavery, but he managed to escape aboard a French ship. Eventually, after still more adventures, he made his way back to England.

For the next couple of years, Londoners saw a short, muscular man with a bristling mustache haunting the city's docks and taverns. The man was the adventurous John Smith, looking for a way to get to America.

Smith finally got to America aboard the *Susan Constant*. Then he became the first person tried by an English court of law in North America.

Writing many years later, Smith said his fellow colonists were jealous of his military reputation. (Smith was never very modest about himself.) He reported that the council accused him of planning to "usurpe [overthrow] the government, overthrow the Councell, and make myself King."

Smith demanded that the council give him a trial by jury. On June 10, the council began Smith's trial. His chief enemy, President Wingfield, felt Smith didn't deserve a trial. But the trial was held, and Smith was found innocent of the charges and allowed to take his place on the council.

Smith's experience and leadership were needed by the new colony. Creating a working colony in the wilderness called for energy and bravery. Smith had these qualities, despite his faults. Unfortunately, few of Jamestown's leaders showed these qualities in the colony's early years.

Most of the colony's "gentlemen," for

*The first major undertaking at Jamestown was the building of a fort.*

example, thought that the hard work of planting and caring for crops was beneath their dignity. Instead, they spent valuable time looking for gold and other riches.

The colonists' first encounter with the local Indians, the Paspaheghs, took place in May. Captain Newport, exploring Chesapeake Bay, landed near a place named Cape Henry. The landing party was attacked by the Indians, and two Englishmen were wounded.

Back at Jamestown, few permanent shelters had been built, and hardly any crops planted. John Smith blamed President Wingfield for a lack of leadership and discipline. This was true in part,

but the settlers didn't have much incentive to work. A few were investors in the Virginia Company, but most were poorly paid employees who had signed a contract to work for seven years.

Jamestown was built on a peninsula—an arm of land in Chesapeake Bay, surrounded by water on three sides. The site was about a hundred miles from the ocean, to avoid attacks by Spanish ships. This made it easy to defend from the Indians, who the colonists knew were watching their every move. Unfortunately, Jamestown was built on marshland, a natural breeding ground for insects that carried malaria and other diseases. The London part of the colony's council had warned of the danger of settling in swampy lowlands. Richard Hakluyt wrote of the dangers: "Neither must you plant in a low or moist place, because it will prove unhealthful." London's instructions also warned the colonists not to build shelters near forests in which "your enemies might hide."

Despite the conflicts in the council and poor relations with the Indians, the Jamestown colonists were optimistic. The land around Jamestown was beautiful, and the weather was pleasant. One of the first settlers wrote, "Such a baye, ryvar and a land did never they eye of man behold."

Although many of the colonists went looking for gold, few ventured very far from Jamestown. Relations with the Indians had improved after the attack at Cape Henry. Indians around Jamestown actually greeted the settlers with a feast and gave them gifts of corn and tobacco.

Captain Newport hoped to make friends with the Indians, but this wasn't easy. There was rivalry among local tribes. Making friends with one tribe usually meant making another an enemy.

The situation became worse in early June. Two hundred Indian warriors attacked Jamestown, killing an English boy and wounding several settlers.

The attack came when Captain Newport, John Smith, and twenty-two colonists had been exploring the James River. On their return, Smith decided to strengthen the fort at Jamestown, adding "four or five pieces of artillerie [cannon]."

A few years before, Jamestown was the sight of a Native American village called Paspahegh, which was also the name of one of the local tribes. The area around Jamestown was home to about forty or fifty Indian tribes. Most of them spoke the Algonquian language. They were not joined into one nation. But two powerful Native American leaders worked to join these many tribes together. If they had been successful, some historians believe, there might have been a powerful Indian nation in North America, like the Aztec Empire in Central America. The two chiefs were Powhatan, leader of a tribe of the same name, and his brother Opechancanough. Since about 1571, the two brothers had conquered many lesser tribes. Eventually, they ruled thirty-two tribes in the Chesapeake Bay region.

John Smith and other colonists described Powhatan with awe. He had great dignity and intelligence, and he ruled more people than some European princes. Smith wrote to England, saying the Indians had an organized society with laws, religion, and agriculture.

On June 14, 1607, several of Powhatan's Indians arrived at Jamestown. They said the recent attack on the Englishmen had come from a minor tribe, not from Powhatan himself. The Indians told the Englishmen to cut down the weeds around Jamestown. That way the settlers could see attackers coming.

A week later, Captain Newport

sailed back to England. His ships carried cedar logs and sassafras root, which was prized as a medicine in England. But Newport had no gold and no report of a passage to Asia. He would not return for seven months.

When Newport next arrived at Jamestown, he brought new settlers for the colony. Some were goldsmiths to work with the gold the settlers were expected to find.

In his 1624 book *The Generall Historie of Virginia*, John Smith wrote that there was "no talke, no hope, no worke, but dig gold, wash gold, refine gold. . . ."

Unfortunately, there was no gold at Jamestown. The settlers had found only the glittering rock called "fool's gold."

Newport discovered that the situation in Jamestown had gone from bad to worse. The long, hot summer along the James River had spread disease among the colonists. The colony had no well, so the settlers drank dirty river water, further spreading illness. With little fresh food, the colonists's diet was poor, too. Daily rations consisted of a little wheat or barley that was full of worms. By August, the hot climate and clouds of disease-carrying mosquitoes were taking a terrible toll in human life.

By September, half of the original 105 settlers were dead. Indian attack had claimed several lives. Many others had died from disease. One had been executed for treason by order of the council. John Smith later wrote that "God (being angrie with us) plagued us with such famin and sicknes that the living

**POWHATAN**
*H eld this ftate & fafhion when Capt. Smith was deliuered to him prifoner 1607*

*This engraving of Powhatan appeared in John Smith's* Generall Historie of Virginia.

were scarce able to bury the dead."

In December 1607, a month before Newport's return, Smith led a trading and exploring party from Jamestown. A band of hostile Indians led by Opechancanough surprised Smith and his men along the Chickahominy River. Two of Smith's men were killed and he was

*The Indians and the settlers meet at Jamestown.*

captured. Smith was taken to the village of Werowomoc and brought before Powhatan.

There are several versions of what happened next. In a June 1608 letter to a friend in London, Smith simply said that Powhatan treated him politely and sent him back to Jamestown. But in a second version in his *Generall Historie of Virginia*, Smith told a different story.

Smith wrote that when he was brought before Powhatan, the Indians argued about what to do with him. Then large stones were brought before Powhatan. Smith was dragged forward and his head "put between the stones."

Two warriors with clubs were about to begin bashing Smith's brains out when Powhatan's young daughter, Pocahontas, ran up. Pocahontas, only eleven or twelve years old at the time, saved Smith's life by placing herself between the Englishman and the warriors.

Whichever version of the story is true, Smith formed an alliance with the chief. Powhatan made Smith a Weroance (chief), and a special relationship grew between the two warriors. Smith's writings show his respect for Powhatan. Still, Smith believed that only force could keep the Indians from destroying Jamestown. He wrote that Powhatan's friendship would turn to treachery if the colonists appeared weak in the face of Indian threats.

Smith's friendship with Powhatan had one important result. The Jamestown settlers began to trade with the Indians for corn and game. Without this

*This engraving illustrates John Smith's story of how Pocahontas saved his life.*

food, the entire colony might have perished.

While Smith was exploring, the colony's council was reduced by several deaths: Bartholomew Gosnold died of malaria, and George Kendall was executed for treason. The council voted to replace President Wingfield with John Ratcliffe, but Ratcliffe proved unable to do the job. Also, Captain Gabriel Archer, an enemy of Smith, became a member of the council.

When Smith returned to Jamestown, Archer ordered him arrested. Smith was

*This beautifully colored map of Virginia, published in London in the 1650s, was based on John Smith's famous map.*

accused of being responsible for the deaths of two of the colonists during the exploring expedition.

As usual, luck was with John Smith. On the same day Smith was arrested, Captain Christopher Newport arrived at Jamestown with supplies. Newport ordered Smith released.

A few days later, Jamestown's fort and many of the settlers' houses were destroyed in a fire. The colony once again needed help from Powhatan. Smith and Newport traveled to the chief's village with goods to trade for corn. In order to help keep the peace while the settlement was rebuilt, the Native Americans and settlers exchanged hostages. This was a common practice of the day. By sending members of one group to live with another, both

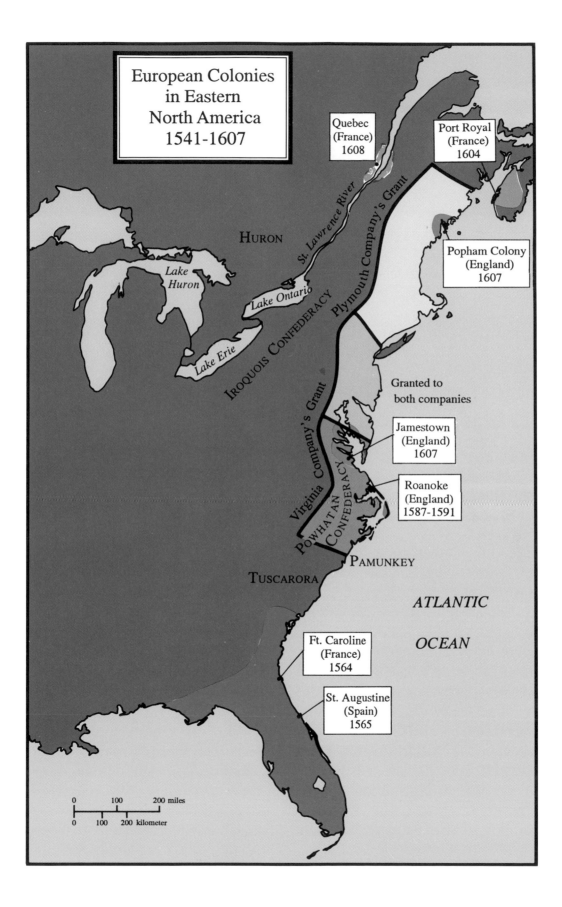

European Colonies
in Eastern
North America
1541-1607

Quebec
(France)
1608

Port Royal
(France)
1604

Popham Colony
(England)
1607

HURON

*St. Lawrence River*

*Lake Huron*

*Plymouth Company's Grant*

*Lake Ontario*

*Lake Erie*

IROQUOIS CONFEDERACY

Granted to
both companies

*Virginia Company's Grant*

Jamestown
(England)
1607

POWHATAN CONFEDERACY

Roanoke
(England)
1587-1591

PAMUNKEY

TUSCARORA

*ATLANTIC*

*OCEAN*

Ft. Caroline
(France)
1564

St. Augustine
(Spain)
1565

0    100    200 miles
0    100    200 kilometer

made sure the other would think twice before attacking.

Powhatan gave the Englishmen an Indian named Namontack, who would be taken to England by Captain Newport. He was exchanged for Thomas Savage, a thirteen-year-old boy. For many years, Savage served the colonists and Native Americans as an interpreter.

Newport loaded his ship with iron ore, cedar and walnut lumber, and sassafras, and set sail for England once again.

In June 1608, Smith began a series of exploring trips with Jamestown as his base. He spent June exploring the coast and islands of vast Chesapeake Bay, journeying up the Rapahannock River as far as present-day Fredericksburg, Virginia.

Smith used the results of his trips to draw the first of several important maps of the new land. His map of Virginia, first published in London in 1612, was so accurate that it was used to settle a border dispute between Maryland and Virginia in 1873.

Returning to Jamestown in September, Smith was elected president of the colony's troubled council. He replaced John Ratcliffe, who had been weakened by sickness.

From September 1608 to August 1609, it was Smith's turn to bring order to Jamestown. It was no easy task. Smith realized that the colonists had to work for survival instead of looking for gold or new routes to Asia. He was a strict leader and established what was practically a "work or starve" policy.

Smith put everyone to work. Gentlemen of noble birth were required (many of them for the first time in their lives) to cut wood, dig ditches, and care for crops.

In October 1608, Captain Newport arrived with more supplies and colonists. Among them were the first women at Jamestown: a Mistress Forest and her maid, Ann Burras. The new group also included the first non-English colonists at Jamestown: three men from Poland and one from Switzerland. They were to teach the colonists important skills, including how to make glass and iron. The four "foreigners," unfortunately, plotted to overthrow Smith and take over Jamestown. They traveled to Powhatan and tried to win the chief's support for the scheme. The plot failed, but Smith was unable to capture the four men.

Smith began a glassworks and ordered a new, stronger fort built. Besides the fort, Jamestown now had a "palisade" of upright logs as protection from attack. Within these walls were the settler's houses. They were of "wattle and daub" construction—twigs woven together to form walls, which were then covered with clay or mud to keep out the wind and rain. Smith also had the colonists dig freshwater wells.

Captain Newport also brought instructions from the Virginia Company in London. Aware of Powhatan's importance as a leader, the company directors told Smith to hold a ceremony and crown Powhatan "king" of his people in the name of King James of England.

*The crowning of Powhatan.*

Smith asked Powhatan to come to Jamestown. Powhatan replied that if he was such a great king, the Englishmen could come to him. So Newport, Smith, and others put on their best uniforms and journeyed to Powhatan's village. There they gave the chief gifts sent from England, among them a gold crown, a red cloak, and an English bed.

Smith later wrote that there was "foule trouble" when the time came for Powhatan to accept the crown. The proud chief refused to kneel, thinking the ceremony might be part of a plot to kill him. Finally, he bent forward a little and allowed the crown to be placed on his head. Powhatan liked the red cloak better; he gave Newport his own fur cape in exchange.

London's instructions raised a more difficult issue, however. The company had spent a lot of money on the colony, and its directors wanted some kind of return on their investment. Newport

*John Smith demands that Powhatan give food to the hungry colonists.*

When you send again, I intreat [ask] you [to send] 30 carpenters, husbandmen [farmers], fishermen, blacksmiths, masons, and diggers of tree's roots . . . rather than a thousand of such as we have.

After Captain Newport's departure, Smith dealt with Jamestown's Indian neighbors much more harshly. He looked on the Native Americans through the eyes of a frontiersman and soldier, not a London gentleman.

As the first snows fell in December 1608, Smith and Powhatan met again. The aging chief asked Smith for some men to build him a house. Smith did so, sending fourteen Englishmen to Powhatan's village, Werewocomoco.

When Smith followed to get some precious corn for Jamestown, however, Powhatan was less friendly. He accused Smith of lying to him about the Englishmen's "visit" to his country. "Many do inform me," Powhatan protested, "that your coming [here] is not for trade, but to invade my people and possess my country."

Powhatan was right. The colonists had told the Indians that they had been defeated by the Spanish at sea and forced to land in Virginia, and that their stay was only temporary.

Powhatan and Opechancanough hadn't been fooled. They had seen English ships come and go from the colony. What's more, about a dozen Indians had been killed by colonists in the six months since Newport's departure. Still more were wounded or jailed at Jamestown. Relations between the

was ordered not to return unless he brought back one of the three things. They were a lump of gold, information about a passage to the "South Sea," or a survivor of Walter Raleigh's lost colony. Also, Newport had to return with local products equal to the cost of the voyage. If he didn't meet these conditions, the colonists would be left to fend for themselves.

Newport sailed home without any of the things the company wanted. But he carried a stern message from John Smith, asking for better colonists:

settlers and the Indians were quickly going bad.

In January 1609, Smith again tried to get food from the Indians. He found Opechancanough and forced him to fill a small boat with corn. Before going back down the river to Jamestown, the fiery Englishman told the Indians they had to load his boat with corn whenever he asked. If not, he would fill it with their "dead carcasses." It was now clear that the colonists and the Indians were in a death struggle.

Such tactics were harsh, but they allowed Smith to keep Jamestown fed. Under Smith's tough leadership, only eighteen of the two hundred or so colonists died in the winter of 1608–9. (Eleven drowned while looking for food without Smith's permission.)

Meanwhile, back in England, the Virginia Company got a new charter. It was now "The Treasurer and Companie of Adventurers and Planters of the City of London for the Firste Colonie in Virginia." Rather than letting the council at Jamestown elect its own president, the new charter called for "one able and absolute governor" to be chosen by the company in London.

Lord De La Warr, a respected nobleman, was appointed "Lord Governor and Captain General." Thomas Smith, a London merchant, was named treasurer. Sir Thomas Gates became deputy governor. He would govern the colony until De La Warr arrived in Virginia.

In May 1609, the company sent nine ships from London. They carried Gates, Sir George Somers (the company's ad-

NEVVES FROM *VIRGINIA.*

THE LOST FLOCKE *TRIUMPHANT.*

With the happy Arriual of that famous and worthy knight S$^r$ *Thomas Gates:* and the well reputed and valiant Captaine M$^r$. Christopher Newporte, and others, into England.

With the maner of their distresse in the Iland of Deuils (otherwise called *Bermoothawes*) where they remayned 42. weekes, and builded two Pynaces, in which they returned into *Virginia.*

BY R. RICH, *GENT.*, ONE OF THE VOYAGE.

LONDON
Printed by *Edw: Allde*, and are to be solde by *Iohn Wright*, at Christ-Church dore. 1610.

*The title page of a 1610 book describing the wreck of Gates and Newports' fleet and their voyage to Jamestown.*

miral), and five hundred new colonists for Virginia. It was the largest expedition to date, and it quickly ran into trouble.

In July, a huge storm struck. One ship sank. A few, carrying about four hundred settlers, struggled on to Jamestown. But the fleet's flagship, the *Sea Venture*, was wrecked on the islands of Bermuda. Those stranded on the Atlantic islands included Gates, Somers, and Christopher Newport.

The *Sea Venture*'s survivors (about

*A colonist's body is carried to Jamestown's burial ground during the winter of 1609–10.*

sixty men) managed to build two small ships from the big ship's wreckage. In them they sailed to Jamestown, arriving in August.

Among the storm's survivors were John Ratcliffe and Gabriel Archer, John Smith's bitter enemies. Immediately after reaching Jamestown they tried to remove Smith as council president. The settlers were loyal to Smith, however, and he stayed in command.

In September, Smith went exploring again. This time he headed northwest, near what is now Richmond, Virginia. Deciding the region would make a better site for a colony than Jamestown, he bought some land from the local Indians.

Unfortunately, a bag of gunpowder exploded near Smith on the way back to Jamestown. He was injured so seriously that he had to return to England for surgery. In October, he sailed for home with what was left of the company fleet.

Smith's departure proved to be a disaster for Jamestown. The new president, George Percy, was described as a brave and honorable man, but he was a poor leader. As the weather grew cold, disaster struck the colony.

The winter of 1609–10 became known as "the starving time." When spring returned, 340 of Jamestown's approximately 400 colonists were dead from hunger, cold, and disease. The few survivors abandoned the colony. They were so weak they might have died if Lord De La Warr hadn't arrived on Sunday, June 16, 1610. De La Warr's first act, it has been written, was to fall to his knees and offer a prayer of thanksgiving.

Jamestown had survived. John Smith made one more trip to North America. In 1614, he led an expedition that surveyed the coast of what Smith named "New England." But Captain Smith—who had done so much to keep the colony alive—never returned to Jamestown.

# 4

## DEMOCRACY, SLAVERY, AND MORE BLOODSHED

Lord De La Warr, Jamestown's savior and new governor, wrote home of his arrival on June 10, 1610: "I caused my commission to be read . . . and then I delivered some few wordes unto the company."

De La Warr's words were stern. He warned the colonists that misbehavior and laziness would cause him to "draw the sword of justice."

Jamestown was in a state of terrible disrepair. De La Warr, a tough old soldier, set out to overhaul the colony. He ordered his men to repair the fort's palisades (log walls) and begin rebuilding the town itself.

Repairs, however, couldn't solve all of Jamestown's problems. Colonists continued to die from malaria and typhoid fever, and from continuing attacks by the Indians. Lord De La Warr

*Lord Thomas De La Warr.*

himself came down with fever about six months after arriving at Jamestown and sailed back to England.

In London, the Virginia Company heard once again that Jamestown needed strong, willing workers instead of the lazy fortune hunters and convicts sent out before. John Smith had said this to the company's leaders, and now De La Warr, Sir Thomas Gates, and Sir Thomas Dale agreed. A new shipment of colonists was recruited.

Gates returned to Virginia as deputy governor, and Dale was appointed to a new post as marshal of Virginia. Dale sailed to Jamestown in March 1611 with "three ships, three hundred people, twelve kine [cattle], twenty goats, and all things needed for the colony." Gates followed in May with three hundred more colonists.

Disappointed by the lack of economic rewards from the colony, the Virginia Company made Dale the virtual ruler of the colony for the next few years. Dale believed the colonists needed strict discipline. The Virginia Company drafted a book of rules and regulations titled *Lawes and Orders, Dyvine, Politique, and Martiall for the Colonye of Virginia*. These "Dale's Laws" called for harsh punishments for colonists who broke them. Whipping was the common punishment for small crimes. In addition to murder, the death penalty could be used to punish rape, adultery, theft, lying, and blasphemy. The Jamestown colonists called Dale's term as Jamestown's marshal (from 1611 to 1616) "five years of slavery."

But along with the new laws, the Virginia Company introduced private ownership of land in Virginia. Until this ruling, no one settler could buy, sell, or harvest his own land. Before, all the colonists contributed the products of their work to the common company store. They had no reason to try and make Jamestown profitable, because any profits went to London, not to the colonists themselves.

Dale gave several acres of land to each of the settlers. They were allowed to plant whatever they wanted and to keep any profit from the sale of their crops. Later, there was a tempting offer to attract new colonists: Each settler who paid his own passage to Jamestown got fifty acres of land, plus fifty more for each person he brought with him. This grant of land was called the "headright" system. By giving people a reason to come to Jamestown, and work

hard once they got there, Jamestown's leaders helped bring free enterprise to North America.

Strict government and free land played a role in Jamestown's eventual success. So did the need for safety, which meant reducing the threat of Indian attack—not only for Jamestown, but for the other settlements that were springing up along the James and York rivers.

Powhatan's warriors continued to harass the colonists. Dale and Gates decided to strike back. Armed settlers destroyed Native American houses and food and took some Indians prisoner. But the attacks went on.

In 1613, after two years of on-and-off warfare, Dale and Gates agreed to a plan offered by Captain Samuel Argall. Argall proposed a devious way of bringing Powhatan to terms: kidnapping "Powhatan's delight and darling, his daughter Pocahontas."

The young woman who had saved John Smith's life (or so he claimed) was now living with the Potomac Indians. The Potomacs were not under Powhatan's control and had good relations with the colonists. The tribe's chief agreed to turn Pocahontas over to the settlers in return for a bribe. Argall then demanded that Powhatan return some English settlers he had taken prisoner, and some tools and weapons he had taken from the colony, if he wanted his daughter returned to him safely. Powhatan finally agreed to free a few hostages, and he sent a canoe full of corn to Jamestown.

*A nineteenth-century painting depicts the marriage of Pocahontas and John Rolfe.*

This didn't satisfy the colony's leaders. Dale, Argall, and some soldiers sailed up river to Powhatan's village with Pocahontas on board. They gave the chief a challenge: He could either fight for his daughter's freedom or return all English prisoners and weapons and give the colony five hundred bushels of corn.

While negotiations dragged on, the colonists sailed back to Jamestown, taking Pocahontas with them. Then an unexpected solution presented itself.

John Rolfe, described as "a gentleman of approved behaviour," said he loved Pocahontas and asked the colony's leaders for permission to marry her. Such a marriage was extremely unusual, and the authorities gave permission only after Pocahontas had been baptized as a Christian.

Rolfe and Pocahontas were married in April 1614. Powhatan refused to attend, but he gave his permission and sent one of Pocahontas's uncles to give the bride away. This marriage of an

*A nineteenth-century engraving shows John Rolfe about to inspect his tobacco plants.*

English man and an Indian woman helped make the next few years peaceful ones at Jamestown.

However, John Rolfe's greatest contribution to Jamestown was not as Pocahontas's husband but as a pioneering planter. In 1611, the pipe-smoking Rolfe had begun experimenting with tobacco plants. The local Indians grew their own tobacco, but it was described as "poore . . . and of a byting taste." Rolfe imported seeds of sweeter tobacco from the West Indies, mixed them with local varieties, and planted it in the rich Virginia soil. He sent samples of the result to England, where smoking was becoming popular. England and Europe loved the new variety, and Jamestown finally had a product it could raise and sell.

In 1615, the colony sent home 2,000 pounds of tobacco. As demand rose, so did production: 20,000 pounds were exported in 1617, 60,000 in 1622, and a whopping 1.5 million pounds in 1629.

Virginia had found gold in the tobacco plant. But tobacco planting was not seen as a blessing by everyone. Many settlers stopped growing corn and food crops and planted tobacco, putting Jamestown's food supply in danger. Governor Dale ordered all landowners to plant at least two acres of corn for themselves and each servant. Those who didn't had to turn over all their tobacco to the colony.

In England, King James strongly objected to his subjects' new habit of smoking. He published a pamphlet called *A Counter Blaste to Tobacco*, in which he described smoking as "A custome loathsome to the eye, hatefull to the nose, dangerous to the lungs."

Despite the royal protest, there was no stopping Virginia's "tobacco madness." With the success of tobacco as an export product, Jamestown's survival was finally assured.

In 1616, John Rolfe, Pocahontas (now called Rebecca), and their young son Thomas sailed to England. The Native American princess quickly became the toast of London. Although King James was reportedly offended that Rolfe, a commoner, hadn't asked him for permission to marry royalty, the Rolfes were presented at his court.

The visit was a great success in interesting people in Jamestown's progress. The Virginia Company used the Rolfes' fame to promote settlement in Virginia and sell the colony's tobacco.

Then, tragically, Pocahontas fell ill and died in London in March 1617. John Rolfe returned to his tobacco plantation the same year.

The year 1619 proved to be a fateful turning point both for Jamestown and the land that would one day become the United States.

The first important event happened because of changes in the Virginia Company's leadership. In April 1619, the company sent out Sir George Yeardley to oversee new policies at Jamestown. These policies, together called the "Great Charter," did away with the harsh "Dale's Laws" and gave more generous land grants to settlers. It also called for a commission to set up a legislative assembly.

There were to be two "Supreme Councils" in Virginia. One would consist of the governor and his counselors, who were chosen by the company. The other council was to be elected by the male colonists. Both councils had to obey the Virginia Company, and ultimately the king. Still, for the first time, settlers would be able to choose at least some of the people who would govern them.

*This portrait of Pocahontas, also called Rebecca, was painted in England.*

On July 30, 1619, the assembly met in Jamestown's log church. John Rolfe wrote to John Smith in London: "Our governor and councell caused burgesses [representatives] to be chosen in all places, and met at a generall assembly, where all matters were debated . . . for the good of the Colony."

Rolfe's letter also noted that "About the last of August a Dutch man of war [ship] came in and sold us twenty Negars [Africans]." The Africans had been captured by slave traders in Africa and sold to the Spanish to work in their colonies in the West Indies. The Dutch

*The first meeting of the Virginia House of Burgesses on July 30, 1619.*

ship had then captured them from the Spanish and brought them to Jamestown.

Desperately short of workers, the colonists quickly bought the Africans from the Dutch. Governor Yeardley himself bought fifteen of them to work on his plantation. Not much is known about these Africans, the first of hundreds of thousands who would be brought to the colonies against their will. Apparently, they were not considered slaves in the sense of being other people's property. Most historians believe these first African Americans were considered "servants for life" by the English colonists. However, the Dutch ship had brought the seeds of slavery to Virginia.

Other kinds of settlers were arriving in Jamestown. In 1619 and early 1620, the Virginia Company sent about two hundred women to Jamestown. The Company's treasurer, Sir Edwin Sandys, also attempted to increase Jamestown's labor force by sending a hundred "younge boyes and girles that lay starving in the streets" of London as *indentured servants*. This meant they had to work for a master for a specific period of time—several years at least—to pay back the cost of their passage from England. Some indentured servants came to Virginia freely to escape a life of poverty in England. Others were beggars or small-time criminals who were given a choice—passage to Virginia as a servant or jail in England.

There were several types of indentured settlers at Jamestown. *Tenants* worked on a plantation—a large farm— for a given period of time. They were entitled to keep half of their earnings. *Bond servants* belonged completely to their master; he kept all their earnings in return for food, clothing, and shelter. *Apprentices*, who were usually the youngest, had to work seven years as bond servants and another seven as tenants. For all classes of indentured servants, years could be added for "crimes" like disobeying a master.

The indenture system provided cheap labor for Virginia's growing plantations. It also had benefits for the servants. The indenture contract between master and servant was a legal document, and the master had obligations, too. Usually, a master had to give his servant land, tools, and seeds when the servant's indenture time was up. And many indentured servants learned a trade from their masters so they could make a living when they became free.

For most of the seventeenth century, there were many more indentured servants than slaves in England's American colonies. But these indentured servants were eventually freed, and many escaped to the frontier before their indentures were completed. In the second half of the seventeenth century, black workers began to replace white indentured servants as the chief labor force on Virginia's tobacco plantations.

*This print by Howard Pyle shows the first Africans arriving in Jamestown in August 1619.*

As slave traders brought more and more Africans to Virginia, questions arose about the status of these new colonists. Could black people become free after working a certain period of time, like white indentured servants? Were the children of black laborers free? What if a black was baptized as a Christian? (According to English law, Christians were not allowed to make other Christians slaves.)

Many historians believe that at first there was little difference in the way black and white laborers were treated at

*This engraving depicts tobacco plants being pressed, dried, and stored in barrels for the voyage to England.*

Jamestown. After all, almost everyone except the colony's leaders was a "servant" of some sort. Some blacks were freed in Jamestown's early years, and the children of these people apparently remained free. Some even owned property.

But over time, important differences developed in the way law and custom considered black people. In 1662, the House of Burgesses passed a law that made it clear that black people were to be considered servants for life. Five years later, another law stated, "Baptisme doth not alter the condition of the person as to his bondage or freedome." And in the early 1680s, a series of "slave codes" defined the status of black people as slaves. They—and their children—were now considered property, to be bought and sold as their owner wished. A 1680 code lists other laws relating to slaves:

> No . . . slave may carry arms . . . nor go from his owner's plantation without a certificate and then only on necessary occasions, the punishment twenty lashes on the bare back, well laid on. And further, if any Negro lift up his hand against any Christian he shall receive thirty lashes, and if he absent himself . . . from his master's service and resist lawful apprehension, he may be killed.

Records show that there were about 300 black people in Virginia in 1650, and 3,000 by 1681. But by 1708, the black population of Virginia, almost all of whom were slaves, was 12,000 out of a total of 60,000 people. Thus, one Virginian in five was a black slave at the beginning of the eighteenth century.

By 1622, the settlers had enjoyed five years of mostly peaceful relations with the Indians, at first thanks to the marriage of Pocahontas and John Rolfe. But Powhatan died in 1618, and he was

*Theodore de Bry engraved this view of the 1622 massacre at Jamestown.*

succeeded as leader of the major Virginia tribes by his half brother Opechancanough.

The settlers had let their guard down during the peaceful years. Suddenly, in March 1622, Opechancanough struck. His warriors carried out attacks on all of Jamestown's outlying plantations. Indians friendly to the colonists warned Jamestown and its closest plantations, but the attacks took the lives of about 350 settlers.

The attack ended any hope of peace between the English and the Indians in Virginia. Governor Yeardley and his successors began waging a campaign to destroy the Indians, or at least drive them from their homes to lands farther west.

The new hostilities in Virginia touched off a round of difficulties for the Virginia Company. Despite the colony's success, the company had failed as a business. For all its efforts, it never made enough of a profit to satisfy its shareholders.

In 1624, the impatient King James broke up the Virginia Company and made Virginia a crown colony, with a governor appointed directly by him. James did allow the House of Burgesses to continue to meet.

Troubles remained ahead for Jamestown and Virginia, but the colonists had achieved a measure of political and economic freedom. And encouraged by Virginia's example, settlers from England began to arrive in other parts of North America. England was in North America to stay.

# AFTERWORD

---

# THE LEGACY OF JAMESTOWN

The royal colony of Virginia got a new monarch in 1625, when Charles I succeeded James I as king of England. The new king resolved to rule Virginia personally. No longer were Virginia's affairs to be conducted in a "democratical" manner.

While the king didn't formally continue the House of Burgesses, the royal governors found that they could not rule Virginia without the cooperation of the colony's assembly. Royal governors called the assembly together to deal with local matters throughout the 1620s and 1630s.

King Charles granted Virginia and the Atlantic island colony of Bermuda a *monopoly* (sole right) to sell tobacco to England. In asking for the colony's co-

*Sir William Berkeley.*

operation, he addressed "Our trusty and well-beloved Burgesses of the Grand Assembly of Virginia." This official recognition of the House of Burgesses set a precedent for royal relations with the English colonies that were springing up in North America.

Charles I's relations with his own assembly, the English Parliament, got off to a bad start. In 1629, the king dissolved—broke up—Parliament. When Parliament met again eleven years later, the situation grew worse. Religious and political tensions in England exploded into Civil War in 1642. Eventually, an army supporting the Parliament forced King Charles from the throne and set up a commonwealth government led by Oliver Cromwell. In 1649, the leaders of the new English government ordered Charles beheaded.

The hard life of the frontier was the

most immediate concern for English settlers in North America. But events in England had a great impact on its colonies.

Virginia's royal governor, Sir Thomas Berkeley, managed to stay in office from 1642 to 1659. In March 1659, he surrendered to a parliamentary fleet when it arrived at Jamestown. The following year the commonwealth collapsed. England again had a king, Charles II (the son of the executed Charles I), and Berkeley returned to Jamestown.

From 1624 to 1660, Virginia (and Jamestown, its capital) experienced ups and downs in two important areas— economic survival and relations with the Indians.

Virginia had grown enormously. In 1648, the population consisted of 13,000 whites and 300 black slaves. There were plenty of domestic animals, like cattle. Vegetables and fruit were grown. The average export of tobacco reached 1.5 million tons per year. In 1670, Governor Berkeley reported that Virginia's population had grown to 40,000, including 2,000 black slaves and 6,000 white indentured servants. That year the colony exported about 12 million tons of tobacco.

Despite the huge amount of tobacco produced, Jamestown's prosperity declined. Under laws called the Navigation Acts, England maintained a monopoly on trade with its colonies. This meant that the colonies could trade only with England and ship their products only in English ships. Thus, merchants in England could set a low price for Virginia's tobacco and other products— while charging high prices for the manufactured goods the colonists needed. Forbidden to buy and sell with other nations, Virginia's trade was almost wiped out.

Another cause for discontent came in 1673, when King Charles granted two of his favorite nobles, the Earl of Arlington and Lord Culpeper, title to all of Virginia for thirty-one years. This meant that they "owned" Virginia, and the colonists had to pay heavy taxes to the two noblemen.

Relations with the Indians had never really been stable since the attacks of 1622. In 1644, Opechancanough, now said to be about one hundred years old, struck again. As in the earlier conflict, the plantations away from the major settlements were the hardest hit. Between three hundred and five hundred settlers were killed. The settlers struck back furiously, slaughtering hundreds of Indians. The fierce old chief was finally captured and killed.

The Indians sued for peace once more. Under the terms of the treaty that ended the conflict, the Indians were ordered to move away from Jamestown and other settlements near the James and York rivers. Any Indian who wanted to enter the territory had to receive special permission. The settlers set

*In this nineteenth-century engraving, Parliament's fleet arrives to remove Governor Berkeley from office.*

up forts at the "border" of the restricted area to keep Indians out of what had once been their homelands.

By this time, war and diseases brought by the settlers had taken a terrible toll on the Native Americans. By 1700, only about a thousand Native Americans of the Powhatan Confederacy remained. There had been twelve thousand when Jamestown was founded less than a century before.

The last major Indian attacks led to a crisis for Governor Berkeley. In June 1676, a wealthy planter named Nathaniel Bacon, Jr., led a group of Virginia frontiersman in a revolt that came to be called Bacon's Rebellion.

The frontier planters were angry that

*Nathaniel Bacon confronts Governor Berkeley during Bacon's Rebellion.*

group of planters in massacring four-teen Susquehannock Indians, members of a peaceful tribe. Berkeley attempted to quash the uprising by offering to build forts along the frontier. This was not enough for Bacon, whom one historian describes as "the spoiled son of a rich squire who had a talent for trouble." Bacon and his followers marched to Jamestown, where he forced the House of Burgesses to agree to a campaign against the Indians. He also wanted to lead the campaign as commander of the militia, the colony's military force. Governor Berkeley refused this, however, and a brief civil war followed. During the conflict, Bacon burned Jamestown to keep it from falling into the governor's hands.

Bacon fell ill and died on October 18, 1676. Berkeley quickly regained control and executed thirty-seven of Bacon's followers.

By now, there were many other settlements in Virginia, almost all bigger than Jamestown. The House of Burgesses continued to meet in Jamestown's statehouse, until another fire destroyed it in October 1698. The few families left in Jamestown moved away.

Virginia needed a new capital, so the House of Burgesses began meeting at a settlement called Middle Plantation on the peninsula between the James and York rivers. In 1699, Middle Plantation was renamed Williamsburg after England's King William III. With the capital now at Williamsburg, Jamestown slipped quietly into history.

The little fort on a swamp on the

Berkeley strictly enforced the Navigation Acts. They also accused the governor of not protecting them from Indian attacks. When Berkeley's plantation was attacked by Doeg Indians, he led a

James River had never become much more than a village. But the events that took place at Jamestown, England's first permanent colony in North America, were truly turning points.

The establishment in 1619 of an elected assembly—the House of Burgesses—helped make possible the democratic form of government the United States has today. At least partly because of this tradition of democratic government, the first president of the United States, George Washington, was a Virginian. Thomas Jefferson, who drafted the Declaration of Independence and later became president, was also a Virginian. In fact, for thirty-two of its first thirty-six years of existence, the United States had a Virginian president.

Sadly, all of these men had something else in common besides being born in Virginia. Each owned slaves. That evil institution, introduced to North America in the fateful year 1619, is a bitter part of the legacy of Jamestown.

# INDEX

Page numbers in *italics* indicate illustrations

# SUGGESTED READING

Bridenbaugh, Carl. *Jamestown, 1545-1699*. New York: Oxford University Press, 1980.

Gordon, Cyrus H. *Before Columbus*. New York: Crown Publishers, 1971.

Hatch, Charles E., Jr. *The First Seventeen Years: Virginia, 1607-1624*. Charlottesville: University Press of Virginia, 1980.

Hawke, David Freeman. *Everyday Life in Early America*. New York: Harper & Row, 1988.

O'Dell, Scott. *The Serpent Never Sleeps: A Novel of Jamestown and Pocahontas*. New York: Houghton Mifflin, 1987.

Scott, John Anthony. *Settlers on the Eastern Shore, 1607-1750*. New York: Alfred A. Knopf, 1967.

Snell, Tee Loftin. *The Wild Shores: America's Beginnings*. Washington, D.C.: The National Geographic Society, 1974.

Stick, David. *Roanoke Island: The Beginnings of English America*. Chapel Hill: The University of North Carolina Press, 1983.

Waring, Gilchrist. *Three Ships Came Sailing*. New York: Dietz, 1948.

Wertenbaker, Thomas J. *Bacon's Rebellion, 1676*. Charlottesville: University Press of Virginia, 1980.

## About the Author

Carter Smith has written and edited books on American history for Silver Burdett Press and other publishers. His *The Korean War* is an earlier contribution to the *Turning Points in American History* series. Although a native of Mobile, Alabama, Smith's ancestors were Virginians.